PICTURE LIBRARY

WHALES

PICTURE LIBRARY
WHALES

Norman Barrett

Franklin Watts

London   New York   Sydney   Toronto

© 1989 Franklin Watts

First published in Great Britain
   1989 by
Franklin Watts
12a Golden Square
London W1R 4BA

First published in the USA by
Franklin Watts Inc
387 Park Avenue South
New York
NY 10016

First published in Australia by
Franklin Watts
14 Mars Road
Lane Cove
NSW 2066

UK ISBN: 0 86313 814 4
US ISBN: 0-531-10703-5
Library of Congress Catalog Card
Number 88-51515

Printed in Italy

Designed by
Barrett & Weintroub

Photographs by
Survival Anglia
Pat Morris
N.S. Barrett
Miami Seaquarium
Sea Life Park, Hawaii
Ardea (Cover)

Illustration by
Rhoda & Robert Burns

Technical Consultant
Michael Chinery

Contents

Introduction

Whales are the gentle giants of the world's oceans. The blue whale is the largest animal that has ever lived. Most whales are harmless to people when unprovoked, yet humans have very nearly wiped out many kinds of whales.

People have hunted whales for hundreds of years, for their oil, for their meat and for whalebone. The great demand for whale products today is in Japan, the Faroe Islands and Greenland.

△ A southern right whale leaps out of the water. This is called breaching. Right whales are baleen whales. They have no teeth.

There are many species (kinds) of whales. They can be divided into two main types, baleen whales and toothed whales.

Baleen whales have horny plates in their mouth instead of teeth. Fringes of bristles attached to the plates strain food from the water.

Toothed whales live on fish and squid. They can hold their prey in their teeth, but swallow their food without chewing it.

△ Two beluga whales underwater. Belugas, also called white whales, are toothed whales and live in cold northern seas.

7

Looking at whales

The blue whale (below) is the largest animal that has ever lived, bigger than any prehistoric dinosaur.

It averages over 100 tons, the weight of about 30 elephants, the largest land animal.

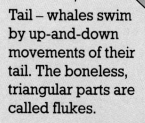

Tail – whales swim by up-and-down movements of their tail. The boneless, triangular parts are called flukes.

Dorsal fin, for stability, small on blue whales, larger on most other whales that have one.

Blow-hole – whales expel used air and breathe fresh air through their blow-hole.

Kinds of whales

Toothed whales have a row of peg-like teeth in each jaw. Baleen whales have horny, triangular plates with frayed inner edges on each side of the upper jaw.

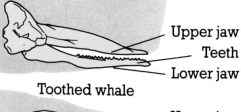

Upper jaw
Teeth
Lower jaw

Toothed whale

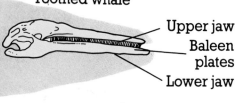

Upper jaw
Baleen plates
Lower jaw

Baleen whale

Flipper – whales have a flipper on each side, used for steering and balancing.

Eye – one on each side of the head.

Whale sizes

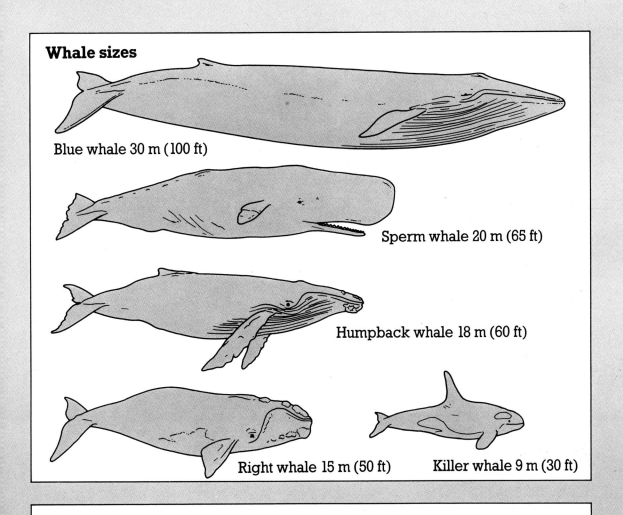

Blue whale 30 m (100 ft)

Sperm whale 20 m (65 ft)

Humpback whale 18 m (60 ft)

Right whale 15 m (50 ft)

Killer whale 9 m (30 ft)

Breathing

A whale comes up to blow out (1) and take in air before diving again (2,3).

Blowing

Experts can identify a whale from the shape and size of the spout it makes.

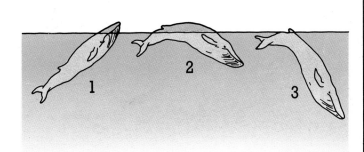

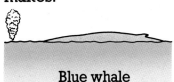

Blue whale

Right whale

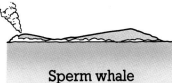

Sperm whale

A very special animal

Whales are mammals. They bear live young, like cats, elephants and human beings. Unlike most other mammals, the majority of whales are hairless and they have only two limbs.

Although whales are like fish in some ways, there are many differences. They have a smooth skin, not scales. Their tail moves up and down, not side to side. Most important, they breathe air.

△ A close up of beluga whales shows their smooth, hairless skin.

▷ An aerial view of a humpback whale shows its flippers clearly. These are its only limbs.

△ A humpback whale with its mouth open, showing the curtains of baleen on each side of its upper jaw, with its tongue in the middle.

◁ Baleen plates from a gray whale. Each plate has a frayed inner edge. Baleen is also called whalebone, although it is not real bone.

Whales have an excellent sense of hearing, even though their ears are barely visible openings just behind the eyes. Toothed whales find their prey by sending out high-pitched sounds. They pick up echoes from anything in the water.

The smaller whales, such as the killer whale and other porpoises, have been studied in captivity. They have been found to be highly intelligent animals.

▽ A scientist examines the body of a dead whale. Under the skin, you can see the thick layer of blubber that helps to keep the whale warm in the coldest waters.

The life of whales

Whales live in all the world's oceans. Apart from humans their only enemy is the killer whale. This is a toothed whale, which sometimes attacks larger whales. Otherwise, whales do not appear to fight among each other. They live peacefully in small family groups, or in larger groups called schools or herds.

Many species of whales migrate (move on) to colder waters in summer to feed. Some species go to warmer waters in winter to breed.

▷ Whales live peacefully in groups. They enjoy playing, and they communicate with each other by means of high-pitched sounds.

▽ A herd of beluga, looking like goldfish under the water. This is a trick of the light, for belugas are pure white, as can be seen from those out of the water.

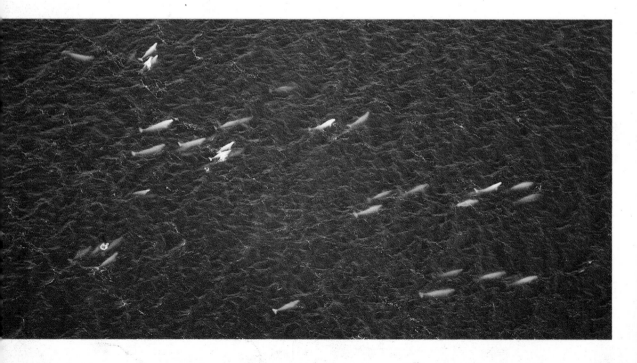

Whales spend most of their time swimming and diving. They often dive, or sound, in search of food. They breathe air at the surface, and hold their breath when they dive. Some whales can stay underwater for over an hour at a time.

Although they breathe air, whales suffocate if stranded on land. Without water to support them, their heavy bodies crush their lungs.

△ Humpback whales feeding at the surface, their upper jaws toward the camera. They feed mainly on krill or zooplankton, as well as mackerel, herring and other small fish.
They take in huge gulps of water as they swim. Their tongue forces out the water while the zooplankton or fish remains on the baleen fringes.

▷ A humpback whale spouting. When a whale is underwater, its breath becomes warm and full of moisture. As the whale blows out at the surface, this moisture, together with cold air condensing as it is struck by the hot breath, forms the spout.

▽ A close up of the blow hole on a gray whale. Patches of barnacles can be seen on the whale's skin. Barnacles are small sea animals that attach themselves to ships and rocks as well as to the larger whales.

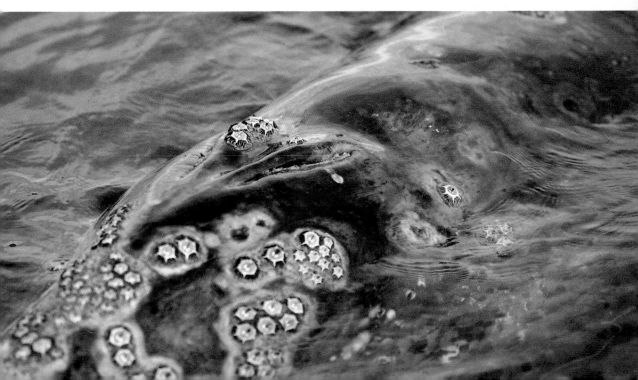

Female whales, called cows, usually have one baby, or calf, at a time. Baleen whales carry their young inside their body for 10 to 12 months, depending on the species. Sperm whales and killer whales are pregnant for 12 to 16 months.

Whales suckle their young on milk that is rich in fat. By the time they are weaned, after about six months, the calves of blue whales, for example, double their length and may be ten times as heavy.

◁ A southern right whale with newborn calf. Baleen cows suckle their young for about six months and are very protective toward their calves. The calves are weaned in rich feeding grounds, where it is easy for them to learn to feed themselves on the zoo-plankton in the water.

▽ A killer whale with her calf, born in captivity.

Baleen whales

There are 11 known species of baleen whales. These belong to three families, the gray whales, the rorquals and the right whales.

There are three species of right whales and only one gray whale. The seven species of rorquals all have prominent grooves on the throat and a tiny dorsal fin further back on the body. They include the humpback whale and the blue whale, which is the biggest of them all.

△ A blue whale at the surface. The blue whale is found in all oceans, but has been hunted almost to extinction.

▷ A gray whale just under the water surface. The gray whale, which lives mostly in the coastal regions of the northern Pacific Ocean and migrates to the lagoons of Baja California in winter, is an endangered species.

△ Humpback whales have very long flippers. They live in all oceans. Whaling has reduced their population from over 100,000 to possibly fewer than 5,000, making them another endangered species.

◁ A southern, or black, right whale feeds at the surface with mouth partly open. Right whales are so called because, in the early days of whaling, they were considered the "right" whales to catch. All species of right whales are endangered.

Toothed whales

There are six families of toothed whales, and nearly 80 species. Except for the sperm whale, they are mostly small to medium size, and include whales commonly called dolphins and porpoises.

There are toothed whales in all the oceans and seas and also in some rivers. Some species have teeth in both jaws, some in just the upper jaw, and others in just the lower.

△ The sperm whale, with its unmistakable large, square-shaped head, is by far the largest of the toothed whales. It lives in all the oceans and can stay underwater for over an hour and dive to depths of 1,000 m (3,300 ft) or more.

Toothed whales can trap and grasp their food. They eat fish and other sea animals. Sperm whales eat mostly squid and some fish.

The killer whale, or orca, is the largest of the porpoises. It lives mainly on fish and squid, but also preys on seals, seabirds and even other dolphins. Groups of killer whales sometimes combine to attack great baleen whales.

△ The pure white beluga whale has a bulging forehead, or "melon." Belugas live in the far north, off Arctic coasts. Their great variety of calls, from clicks and squawks to trills and whistles, earned them the name of sea canary.

▷ The pilot whale, or blackfish, is a type of dolphin. Pilot whales usually live in large groups, following one or more leaders, or pilots. The picture clearly shows the simple, peg-like teeth common to all toothed whales.

▽ The killer whale is the biggest of the porpoises. It is easily recognized by its large dorsal fin.

Saving the whale

Whales are intelligent, harmless animals that have been living peacefully in the world's oceans for 50 million years, until people began to hunt them.

Why do people kill whales? It is only for profit, because none of the things we get from whales is essential to our way of life.

Campaigns to save the whale have met with some success. But some countries continue to hunt whales, and their survival is still seriously threatened.

△ Watching and even touching a gray whale. Whales are fascinating creatures but should be approached with caution and treated with respect.

▷ The dead body of a gray whale, tangled up in fishing gear. Many large whales and dolphins die, unable to reach the surface to breathe, when they are caught in the vast nets set in some parts of the world.

The story of whales

The first whales

The most ancient whales known from fossils swam the seas about 50 million years ago. Many scientists believe they were amphibious, living in the water but breeding on land. Fossil remains also tell us that many features of today's whales, including their streamlined, torpedo shape, developed between 40 and 25 million years ago.

△ An illustration of the Bible story in which Jonah is cast onto land by the whale.

Whales in folklore

Whales have a long history of friendship with human beings in all seafaring civilizations. Stories abound of dolphins rescuing sailors at sea, and giving rides to youngsters.

Perhaps the best known whale story is from the Book of Jonah, in the Bible. Jonah, a Hebrew prophet, is said to have been swallowed up by a whale, or "big fish," after being thrown into the sea by sailors. The whale later cast Jonah onto dry land, and he was able to carry on with his preaching.

The family of whales

Whales make up a group of mammals in the animal kingdom known as cetaceans. It includes the dolphins and porpoises. Cetaceans have a long natural life span, 30 or 40 years, maybe longer. Killer whales have been known to live to 90! So, even with their low birthrate, they have survived comfortably over millions of years – until people began to kill them.

The whaling industry

Men are thought to have hunted whales from canoes thousands of years ago. Whaling on a large scale began in the United States in the 1760s, and by the mid-1800s they had built up a vast whaling fleet.

The great American whaling industry began to decline as kerosene took the place of whale oil as fuel for lamps. But whaling prospered in other countries. A

Norwegian whaler invented the harpoon gun in the 1860s, and steamships began to be used for whaling.

From the 1930s to the 1950s, whales were being killed at the rate of 30,000 a year. As one species became so scarce that it was no longer worth hunting, so another took its place. In 1946, the whaling nations set up the International Whaling Commission (IWC) to regulate the industry. It prohibited or controlled the hunting of certain species. But some countries have continued to ignore or get round the rules.

△ A tin of whalemeat as sold in Japan. Most of the whales now hunted are killed mainly to produce whalemeat for the Japanese, who regard it as a luxury food, served mainly in expensive restaurants. It is also eaten in Norway and Iceland.

△ A modern harpoon gun, a vicious weapon that explodes a grenade inside the whale's body and causes an often agonizing death. The first harpoon gun was invented in the 1860s.

Ending the slaughter

During the 1970s, a world movement gathered enough strength to put an end to the slaughter of whales. Inspired largely by conservationist groups like Greenpeace, a five-year international ban on whaling was introduced in 1986. Still, some countries, notably Iceland and Norway, have bent the rules and continue to kill whales, chiefly for the sale of whalemeat to Japan.

But they are not the only culprits. Many nations pump millions of gallons of industrial waste into the sea, polluting the water and the feeding grounds of the whales. With this serious new threat and the continuation of whaling, we still have a long way to go before we save the whale from extinction.

Facts and records

Big baby blue
The calf of the blue whale measures about 7.3 m (24 ft) and weighs as much as 3 tons (6,000 lb) at birth. Fed on a diet of rich milk, it almost doubles its weight after the first week and then gains 90 kg (200 lb) a day.

△ An engraving, or scrimshaw, on the tooth of a sperm whale.

Scrimshaw
Scrimshaw was a sailor's sparetime handicraft. A common occupation of sailors in old whaling days was to engrave designs on whales' teeth. Scrimshaw engravings made valuable souvenirs.

The singing humpback
The singing of humpbacks consists of a series of vocalizations that can last up to 30 minutes or more. The pattern, varies from season to season. All the whales in the same breeding ground sing the same song, which slowly changes over the season. One remarkable discovery about their song is that they start a new breeding season with the same "tune" they sang at the end of the previous year. The song of the humpback has been recorded and is available on records and tape.

△ The tail of a humpback as it dives underwater. The remarkable underwater "singing" of the humpback has been detected at distances of 185 km (115 miles)

Glossary

Baleen
Horny plates in the mouth of the so-called baleen whales, with fringes that strain food from the water.

Blow hole
The opening through which a whale breathes. Baleen whales have two adjoining blow holes.

Blubber
A thick layer of stored fat under the skin of whales and some other animals.

Cetaceans
The group, or order, of animals containing the whales.

Dorsal fin
A fin on the back of the body.

Extinct
A species is extinct when there are no longer any living specimens.

Flukes
The boneless, triangular parts of the tail.

Fossil
An impression of the remains of an ancient animal or plant, preserved in rock.

Melon
The bulging forehead of some toothed whales and dolphins.

Migrate
To travel from one area to another. Many species of whales migrate to warmer waters to breed, later returning to their original homes to feed.

Right whale
One of a small group of baleen whales, distinguished from rorquals by smooth (ungrooved) throats.

Rorqual
Any member of the family of baleen whales with deep grooves on the throat.

Species
A particular type of animal. Animals of the same species breed young of that species.

Streamlined
Smoothly shaped for moving through water (or air).

Zooplankton
The mass of tiny animal and plant life that lives in the surface layers of the oceans.

Index